An Interview
with
Chiara Lubich

An Interview with Chiara Lubich

by
William Proctor

new city press, new york

© 1983 by New City Press, Brooklyn, N.Y.

All rights reserved. No part of this book may be used or reproduced in any manner whatsoever without written permission, except in the case of reprints in the context of reviews.

ISBN: 0-911782-44-3
Printed and bound in the United States of America

Cover design: Russell Campitelli

Introductory Note

In 1943, in Trent, Italy, Chiara Lubich, a young Catholic, privately consecrated her life to God, with no other purpose in mind than to live for him. Today, forty years later, more than a million people throughout the world, of all ages, vocations, and social backgrounds—Protestants, Catholics, Orthodox, and even Jews, Muslims, and Buddhists—gratefully acknowledge that her life and the spirituality of unity she promotes have had a profound impact on their lives and have brought them closer to God. The majority of these people are in some way part of the Focolare Movement.

The Movement began in the midst of the terrible destruction of World War II. Chiara Lubich realized that God is the only one worth living for and she began to center her life on the Gospel, together with a small group of young women who wanted to follow her. Their ideal became one of striving toward the fulfillment of Jesus' prayer to the Father: "That they all may be one" (Jn. 17:21). Their way of life soon attracted others, men and women, young and old, who began to live the Gospel with them. Thus the Focolare Movement was born. "Focolare" means "hearth," "family fireside." It was the name spontaneously used by people in Trent to describe the love, warmth, and family atmosphere they found among Chiara and her friends. And the movement which was coming to life around them became known as the Focolare Movement.

The life of Chiara and her first companions, and the spiritual way they followed, gave rise to the unique form of spirituality characteristic of the Focolare Movement: the spirituality of unity. It has proved to be a powerful means of introducing the Gospel into modern life, of going to God together. The Focolare Movement was approved by Pope John XXIII in 1962.

Since the movement is frequently mentioned in the course of this interview, the following brief definitions may prove helpful to those readers who are not familiar with it.

Focolare: A Focolare is a small community of celibate and married men or women whose first aim is to achieve among themselves the unity Jesus prayed for, through the constant practice of mutual love. Celibate members live together; married members live with their families. All have normal jobs.

Focolarina: A member of a woman's Focolare. Plural: Focolarine.

Focolarino: A member of a men's Focolare. Plural: Focolarini (also used to indicate Focolarine and Focolarini collectively).

Volunteer: The Volunteers—short for "Volunteers for God"—are members of the Focolare movement who are particularly committed to bringing the Gospel spirit to bear on the relationships and structures of society at large.

Gen: Gen is short for "New Generation," and the Gen Movement is the new generation of the Focolare Movement. The Gen are young people committed to living the Gospel message of love and unity and to sharing with other youth their conviction that Jesus is the answer.

I would like to thank Sharry Silvi for her invaluable assistance during the preparations for this interview and for kindly serving as simultaneous translator during the interview itself.

Foreword

The two words which best sum up the purposes of the Focolare movement are unity and love. And certainly these two concepts, which encompass much of the teaching and work of salvation accomplished by Jesus Christ, represent values of far-ranging—indeed, cosmic proportions.

Yet it's important to realize that an abstract, philosophical understanding of these two terms cannot really capture their essence. On a very fundamental level, unity is a moral value that concerns how well we get along with those who live and work with us. Similarly, love is best defined many times by what it *does*, rather than what it *is*.

St. Paul recognized the connection between the practical imperatives of love and our ability to live and work harmoniously with others when he wrote in 1 Corinthians 13:4-7: "Love is always patient and kind; it is never jealous; love is never boastful or conceited; it is never rude or selfish; it does not take offense, and is not resentful. Love takes no pleasure in other people's sins but delights in the truth; it is always ready to excuse, to trust, to hope, and to endure whatever comes." (The Jerusalem Bible).

It's on this intensely practical level that Chiara Lubich and the Focolare Movement have perhaps the most to contribute. In my discussion with her in Italy and at dinners and other meetings I've had with Focolarini in New York City, I've been impressed by two things: First of all, the Christians in the Focolare movement are eager to test their faith and values in the *real world*—in the pressure-packed milieu of business interactions, urban social tensions and family problems that we all face. Secondly, they are willing to discuss their struggles in this difficult environment and to explain how they have conquered the challenges through Christ.

Whenever we have dinner with the Focolarini in Manhattan, my wife always says, "I expect God is going to show us something new tonight!" And he always does.

 I trust this conversation with Chiara Lubich will also introduce you, the reader, to something new that will help you understand more fully that unity in love which God wants for all of us.

William Proctor

Contents

Introductory Note	5
Foreword	9
Interview	15
Appendix	65

Interview

I've been very interested in reading about your early spiritual experiences, and particularly your experience at the shrine of Loreto at age nineteen. I wonder if you would regard that experience as a complete conversion experience, or was it more like a renewal experience?

It was neither one. It was the discovery of my vocation. If you wish, I could tell you what happened.

It was 1939. I was poor. There was a convention of the Catholic Action in the northern part of Italy and I was invited to attend, all expenses paid. But there was the threat of war and my father said I could not go. Although it was a suffering to have to renounce going, with the help of God's grace I recognized his will in the will of my father and was content not to go. I mention this because it seems to me, from what happened later, that this act of renunciation had pleased Jesus. For, in spiritual matters, all life presupposes a death to self: "Unless a grain of wheat falls into the earth and dies, it remains alone; but if it does, it bears much fruit" (Jn. 12:24).

    Shortly after that, in fact, I was invited to go to another gathering, this time in Loreto, and that turned out to be the most important trip of my life. When I arrived there from Trent, I entered the little House of Loreto, which is set like a pearl in a huge fortress church. Tradition says that this was the house of the Holy Family in Nazareth, and that the angels moved it from place to place, finally leaving it in Loreto. I was deeply moved. I thought of Jesus, Mary, and Joseph, and I imagined them moving about from one place to another in the house. I thought that, perhaps, through the window, which is in the rear of the house, the angel had announced the Incarnation to Mary. Perhaps those walls had resounded with the singing of Mary and the voice of Jesus and had witnessed the work of Joseph. As I leaned against those time-blackened walls, the supernatural almost overpowered me, and I began to cry. This happened repeatedly, because every day I went to that extraordinary place and remained there, immersed in the same contemplation.

The last day, I was at the back of the church which contains the little house. The church was filled with young women wearing white veils. I had a strong feeling that many others would follow me in virginity. I went back to Trent with the conviction that I had found my way in life. It was not the way of a natural family; nor the way of a convent. Neither was it only to live a celibate life, while remaining in the world. Yet it was something which had the beauty of these three vocations. It was a fourth way. It would be a family, yes, but a supernatural one. It would be a convent, a "covening," a coming together of people; but of people who form a family. It would be in the world, yes, but with the totally evangelical life of those who leave their relatives for Jesus and come to live together with others who have the same vocation, thus forming a family of people who live in virginity, like the family of Nazareth, which had dwelled in the house of Loreto.

Later I understood that the Focolare communities are the incarnation of this fourth way, and that, like the family of Nazareth, they have to be composed both of persons who live in virginity and of married people who are in some way consecrated to God.

In the light of your own personal experience, and from the experience of others you have known in the Focolare Movement, how would you define spiritual maturity?

As Christ living permanently—insofar as that is possible here on earth—in the Christian.

What helps us mature spiritually; and what are signs or marks of spiritual maturity?

The sign is one's love of neighbor. From how much a person loves his or her neighbor, you can see how much he or she loves God. To go back to the other question, love of neighbor is what helps us to become mature, because love of neighbor makes our love for God grow. St. Teresa of Avila, whom you probably know of, and St. Catherine of Siena, both of whom are Doctors of the Church, were also convinced of this.

The deeper a plant sends its roots into the earth, the higher it grows. Similarly, the more Christians "make themselves one" with others, the more they love others, the more their love for God increases. This was our experience from the very beginning.

The Lord was strongly urging us to love our neighbor, to love Jesus in him or her. We tried to live like this all day long, making ourselves one with all the persons we met, sharing their joys and their sufferings, making ourselves one with their aspirations, and so on. As a result, when evening came and we recollected ourselves in prayer, we began to experience a certain union with God, even though we were at the beginning of our spiritual life.

Thus we experienced that love of neighbor makes our love for God grow. It is a wellspring of union with God.

Some have said that it takes a long time to become mature, and they might point to

the length of time, perhaps fourteen to seventeen years, that Paul spent in Arabia before he blossomed into full leadership at the Council of Jerusalem. Do you think there is a length of time that a person should count on to become mature?

I think it depends on the program that God has for the particular person. For St. Therese of Lisieux, for instance, relatively few years were enough. And lately we have been speaking about Sister Maria Gabriella of the Trappistine Monastery of Grottaferrata, who offered her life for the unity of the Churches, and whose process of canonization has now begun. At her death, she was already considered a saint by those around her. She had reached perfection in three or four years. Before that, she had been a rough and domineering person.

I would say, however, that for the saints it has generally taken quite a few years. In fact, the spiritual masters say that the dark night of the soul, which is a period of great purification that precedes the so-called spiritual marriage, lasts from five to fifteen years, and may even last up to forty years. But, as I said, for each saint it has been different.

When you say "spiritual marriage," what do you mean?

It is a particular moment in which, according to Catholic experts on the spiritual life, the transformation of the soul into God takes place. God and the soul become one.

You mentioned that that sister had reached perfection. Does that mean she would have experienced the spiritual marriage?

Quite probably, because she made a total offering of herself to God; and self-immolation, accepted by God, is of great value in reaching spiritual maturity.

When you say immolation, that could be understood in the East and elsewhere as actually physically burning oneself up. Is that what you mean?

No. She offered herself to God as a small offering for the unity of the Churches. God accepted, and soon afterward she became sick.

In terms of the outward expression of her perfection, would it be accurate to say that this was a perfect expression of love toward others as well as toward God?

Certainly, because she gave her life for the unity of the Churches.

Do you sense any tension between being the leader of a large movement in the Christian Church and trying to lead a genuine, humble, Christian life yourself?

No, because my primary concern is not so much to lead, as to teach by example. And this prompts me, with the help of God's grace, to live an ever more authentic Christian life.

A great deal is said in and about the Focolare Movement with regard to love and

expressing love. I wonder if you could define what love is?

Love is the mark of a Christian, the specific characteristic of Christianity.

Can you give an illustration as to how one might express love?

The cross. Jesus expressed love, dying for us on the cross.

If you were trying to tell an ordinary person, Christian or non-Christian, exactly what love is, what illustration would you use? Would you say it is a feeling? Or is it something which is expressed in action? Or both?

Love is, above all, sacrificing oneself for others; but it is also a sentiment. It is also the effort to make oneself one with the will of another, to make oneself one with the other. A prototype, on a human level, that could be a symbol of divine love is a mother's love. A mother is filled

23

with the sentiment of love, and her life is characterized by much sacrifice for her children. She is the one who most understands her children and tries to make herself one with them. God has a love of this kind, but, his is much greater.

Do you feel that it's possible to live a genuinely joyful, relaxed, and peaceful life, in terms of your inner life, in today's high-pressured urban environment?

Yes. And I would like to tell you how we find this joy and this inner peace while remaining in the midst of the world, with the noise of telephones, cars, TV, and all the usual clamor. But first, I would like to recount an episode which led us to the key for resolving this problem.

It was the beginning of our new life, and I had gone to visit a friend of mine who was sick. A priest who was there to give her the Eucharist asked me, "Do you know when it was that Jesus suffered the most?" And I answered, "Perhaps it was in the Garden of Olives." At that time, in fact, this was the common belief. The priest answered, "No, Jesus suffered the most when on the cross he cried out, 'My God, my God, why have you forsaken me?' "

When the priest left the room, I turned to my sick friend and to whomever else was there with me and said: "If Jesus suffered the most in his abandonment, then we who want to follow him crucified should choose him as our Ideal in the moment when he cried, 'My God, my God, why have you forsaken me?' We have only one life; let's choose to live it for him!"

I said this because I had great faith in the priesthood: what came from the lips of a priest was taken by me as if it came from God.

From that moment on, all suffering—whether personal, or that of our brothers and sisters, our small community, the Church, or humanity—seemed to us an expression of his suffering, the suffering of Jesus forsaken.

In all the manifestations of suffering we beheld his countenance, especially in spiritual suffering. So when we experienced an inner sadness, for instance, or aridity, or a lack of peace, or the burden of our sins, or a sense of failure, we would find a deeper meaning for all these personal sufferings in his cry.

For, in the moment of his abandonment, Jesus was left in darkness. It seemed that he, who is the Truth, the Light of the world, could not see the Father anymore, the Father who had never abandoned him. In that moment he experienced the greatest possible aridity. He had lost the immense, divine joy of his union with the Father, and felt the burden of all our sins on his shoulders. He felt a failure; peace, tranquillity, and joy were banished from his soul.

Thus, viewing our suffering as a participation in his, we would embrace him forsaken in that suffering. And we would say from the depths of our heart: "This is what I want, this is what I have chosen." Forgetting ourselves, we would plunge into this new adventure and wholeheartedly begin to do whatever was God's will for us in the following moment. And very often, almost always, the sense of aridity and of being without light, peace, and tranquillity would disappear.

This is how we learned to overcome inner difficulties. But that is not all. We also saw the face of Jesus forsaken in the external circumstances that were an obstacle to the peace, joy, and tranquillity of our souls. And so we would accept them and love them as an expression of Jesus—as Jesus. And in accepting and embracing them, we experienced the return of deep, supernatural peace and joy.

A number of people have referred to you and to what you do in terms of having a charism or gift from God. Can you tell me when and how you first realized that you had a special gift from God?

I couldn't tell you the exact moment, but there were a few incidents in 1943 that I remember, and I will tell you about one of them. I was giving philosophy lessons to a young woman, who later became one of my first companions. Her name is Doriana Zamboni. One day I was telling her about the theories of Kant. In my efforts to explain things from his perspective, I began to identify with his ideas, and so did my friend. Suddenly a thought came to me: "This way of thinking is certainly far from the truth of the resurrection of the body!" Hanging above my desk, as a reminder of Jesus' love, was a picture of the Sacred Heart, to whom my family was consecrated. Urged from within, I placed my hand on his heart and said, "I believe in the resurrection of the body, even if I cannot explain it!" I remember that to affirm my faith more strongly, I said, "I *swear* that I believe in the resurrection of the body!"

In that moment, it seemed my mind was opened, and, using analogies, I explained this truth. I don't remember now a word of what I said, but I do remember that this truth of our faith was as clear to me in that moment as the theories of Kant. I understood, then, something which I have seen confirmed repeatedly since: that there is a light which comes from above, an understanding which is not a fruit of our intelligence, but which comes from God.

Later, I'm not sure if it was the same day, I said to my friend, "What should we call this light which comes from above?" And I answered, "The Ideal!" From that moment on, everything concerning our new life, this gift that God has given us—that can now be called a charism because the Church has approved it—as well as the collection of truths that struck us in a particular way and now form our spirituality, have been referred to by us as our "Ideal."

If you had to describe exactly what the "Ideal" consists of; that is, describe the charism in more specific terms, how would you describe it?

I would repeat what I have just said. It is like a light from above, something which enlightens the intellect and motivates the will. It is a light that helps us to a new understanding of the Gospel, the Church's dogmas, and all that concerns God or the Church. For example, the words of the Gospel, "Love your neighbor *as yourself*," "Love one another *as I have loved you*," "*As the Father has sent me...*so I send you" have all acquired new meaning. God really wants us to love our neighbor *as ourselves*; that is, just as willingly and just as much. We understood this at that time and tried to put it into practice.

Some, referring to what Paul says in 1 Corinthians 12, would make precise references to certain types of gifts, like a gift of wisdom or a gift of knowledge, or maybe a gift of evangelism, or a gift of administration. Can you fit your gift into one of those? Or is it something which is separate?

I wouldn't be able to define it, but perhaps it is the gift of wisdom or the gift of understanding.

I think you have touched on this, but I would like to explore it a little more. Would this be an individual gift that you feel you have, or would this be something that others in the Movement also have? Is it something which is embodied in the Focolare Movement as a whole?

It is an individual gift, which, however, is not for one person's benefit alone, but for the benefit of the Church and of humanity. It is embodied in a community, in a Movement in the Church, precisely so that it can be shared with others, and so that as many people as possible may come to understand it and to live accordingly.

Why do you think that God has given you this particular gift at this particular time?

I believe it is because this gift of his highlights everything in the Gospel that has to do with unity and with the way to unity: love for Jesus crucified and forsaken. In today's world we find many divisions. Families are divided by misunderstandings, separations, divorce, and barriers between children, parents, and the elderly. There are also divisions and intolerance in society at large, such as between political parties and opposing factions within nations. There are wars. Racism is still alive. Christianity itself is marked by disunity among the Churches. Christians of different denominations fight one another, as in Northern Ireland. The world is divided; Christianity is divided.

Unity is what needs to be stressed at this moment in history. There are many people who are trying to promote a unity which is not based on God, but rather on atheism and materialism. Therefore, we need to work to bring about a unity founded on spiritual principles.

Do you expect the Focolare Movement to live on after you're gone?

Certainly I do. Perhaps not exactly as it is now, but it will certainly live on. Our strength lies in establishing the presence of Jesus in our midst. The mutual love among the members of the Movement, which leads to unity, brings about this wonderful reality. Jesus is there where two or more are united in his name, which means united by his love. If, in the future, Jesus is always present among the leaders of the Movement, and in our Focolares, our Gen units, the nucleuses of the Volunteers, and in all our communities and families, he will be their light, he will lead them on. In fact, even now, he is the one who gives life to our Movement, who sustains it and leads it, because with his presence he enlightens us, purifies us, sanctifies us, spurs us on.

What is the most difficult problem you face now?

No problem is difficult when we have Jesus crucified and forsaken before us.

What about the future; is there one that you anticipate?

Perhaps when I leave this world, the Movement will experience some difficulty. They say that when founders die, the movements or works they have founded go through a sort of dark night. We are trying, however, to prepare ourselves for that moment, and if the spirit of the Movement continues to be alive in the Focolarini, that trial will be overcome.

How are you trying to prepare for that? Are you grooming certain leadership, or is it something else?

We have a Rule which provides that when the founder or president of the Movement dies, there is to be an assembly, and elections are to be held. Thus, the Movement's life will go on. As for me, I always try to keep in mind, as an example, a person about whom I read many years ago. She was a fairly young woman, who had ten children, some of whom were very small. She discovered that she had cancer and was told that she would die within a few months. With extraordinary determination, she managed to find homes for each of her children in ten different families. You can imagine what she must have gone through as she was doing this, and especially when she went to visit all her children for the last time. But at last, when the end was near and she lay on her deathbed, she said: "Everything is in order."

I, too, would like to leave everything in order. So I want to gather all we have written or said about our spiritual experience during these thirty or forty years—or however many there will be. In this way, those who come after me will be able to go back and see what the first ideas were that God gave us about this Movement.

What gives you the greatest happiness now? I mean, you seem to be a happy person anyhow, but is there something which gives you more happiness than anything else?

The moments of greatest happiness in my life are the moments in which, because of God's grace, I realize how much he loves me.

As a leader, are you able to find others with whom you can share in depth your problems and concerns?

Yes, because communion and unity are our way of life. So it is natural for us to share with one another. It is almost second nature. In fact, we do not consider it an act of mortification to leave our solitude to go out toward others, but rather to leave the wonderful atmosphere of the community where Christ lives in our midst, to do something on our own.

You said, "mortification"?

Yes, because it involves suffering, letting go of something. We are often reminded of something St. Catherine of Siena said, which is that sometimes we have to leave God for God. We have to leave God, who has been present among us, to go and do his will.

I would imagine that as the founder of the Movement, even if you are able to share in depth with others, you probably tend to give more than you receive. And I wonder if, in that process, you ever feel spiritually drained or exhausted?

Absolutely not! Because this process of giving and receiving is one that takes place not between us and others, but between us and God. From the very beginning, we experienced the truth of Jesus' words, "Give, and it will be given to you. A good measure, pressed down, shaken together and running over, will be poured into your lap" (Lk. 6:38). Since, when we give, it is not merely to human beings but to God, he is the one who repays us. So we are constantly receiving. When we give out of love for him, he fills us with himself.

When you say he gives back to you, what happens exactly? Is it a feeling you have? Or what?

I would call it supernatural joy. But it is also light that enables me to see what I should do. Our life is both contemplative and active.

What is the primary source of your own spiritual strength? Maybe you just answered this, I don't know.

Loving God and loving my neighbor. I love God by trying to do his will completely, by wanting his will, by living in conformity with his will, and especially by making myself one with his will and telling him, "I want what you want." In this way, my soul becomes filled with joy, a real supernatural joy which is a source of spiritual strength and light. And, as I said, when we love our neighbor, our union with God grows. This union gives us extraordinary spiritual strength.

How would you compare what you are doing in the Focolare Movement with some other Christian movements, like the Franciscans or the present-day Charismatics?

If we look at these movements which have arisen in the Church, we find that their spirituality can frequently be expressed in a single word. Franciscans certainly have love as their aim, but the way God has given them to achieve this is the way of poverty. With the word "poverty," one can express the whole Franciscan spirituality. And if we look at St. Benedict, we see that his spirituality is concentrated in the words, "Pray and Work" (*Ora et Labora*). Similarly, the word which most expresses St. Ignatius is "obedience." St. Therese of Lisieux has her "little way." St. Catherine of Siena expresses her spirituality in two words: "blood and fire." And the word "prayer" sums up St. Teresa of Avila's spiritual way.

As you see, there are different ways to live the Gospel, each with its respective charism. God has given these charisms to the world through movements and religious orders as answers to the needs of the Church and of humanity at particular moments in history.

It seems to me that the Charismatic Movement today emphasizes prayer and various spiritual gifts in the Church.

If one word could express the gift that God has given to the Focolare Movement, that word would be "unity." We want to bring about unity through love.

Do you feel it is possible to have progress in Christianity, or to achieve something new, or to expand our spiritual horizons in a new way?

Yes, because the Holy Spirit is always at work; and the Holy Spirit is light and revelation. He leads us to a deeper understanding of the truth, particularly—we Catholics believe— through the popes, the bishops and the councils. The Holy Spirit also brings this about through the work of theologians, as well as through the faithful, whose charisms must be verified by the Church.

Do you think it is ever possible to add to fundamental truths as we go along, or have these truths been laid down once and for all, let's say in Scripture?

These truths have been laid down once and for all. We cannot add to them. Everything is there already. Nevertheless, they are always open to greater clarification and deeper understanding. For example, the charism God has given to the Focolare Movement and the life based on this charism have led to a deeper understanding of certain truths; they have shed new light on the meaning of Jesus' "testament," his priestly prayer. What the Movement has particularly stressed is that these words of Jesus can become a reality in our lives, and that the key to unity is the mystery of Jesus crucified and forsaken. But this is only one example.

You talk about unity. Can you explain how you go about it, how Catholics can work first of all with other Christians (Protestants, Orthodox, and so on), and also with non-Christians in achieving this sort of unity? How can this happen without compromising basic convictions?

First of all, we must distinguish between the unity that Catholics can achieve with other Christians and the unity they can achieve with the faithful of other religions. In the Movement, of course, we always work to achieve whatever unity is possible. With Protestants there are immense possibilities. We have the same baptism, the same Christ, the same Holy Spirit. We all belong to the same Mystical Body, though perhaps in slightly different ways; we believe in Sacred Scripture; and so on.

In the Movement, we stress all these things we have in common. For instance: Protestants, too, want to put into practice Jesus' New Commandment, and we do this with them, ready to die for one another. This has tremendous consequences: Jesus establishes his presence among us and we can bear witness to him together. That this witness is a reality is proven by many examples from our life. I will give you one. Around 1960, after getting to know some non-Catholic Christians in Germany, we started to have meetings with Catholics and Lutherans together in Rome. One of these meetings was particularly successful because of a special grace. A tremendous joy filled everyone. Three Anglican priests who happened to be present were deeply struck. Their reaction was: "If Catholics are accomplishing such deep unity with Lutherans, they will be able to have an even deeper unity with Anglicans, with whom they have greater bonds." And they concluded: "We want to return with other Anglicans—perhaps an entire planeload." This is exactly what happened. In this way the Movement developed among the Anglicans in England where it is now flourishing. There are now about ten thousand Anglicans and several Anglican bishops who are close to the Movement. Anglican interest in the Movement also resulted from the fact that while Archbishop Ramsey was Archbishop of Canterbury, he became interested in the Movement, as did his successors, Archbishop Coggan and the present primate, Archbishop Runcie.

This kind of [united Christian] witness is a daily occurrence at Ottmaring, near Augsburg, Germany, where we have an ecumenical center, a small town where Lutherans and Catholics live together. The Catholics belong to the Focolare Movement, and the Lutherans, for the most part, belong to *Bruderschaften*, communities of both married and celibate members, some of whom live a community life. At Ottmaring, all pray together and put into practice the Word of Life, month by month, as is commonly done throughout the Movement. And, above all, they love one another as Jesus has commanded us to do. This small town gives a truly powerful witness. Both the Catholics and Lutherans there feel that it belongs to both groups. Ottmaring has become a common ground where both Catholics and Protestants feel at home and where Catholic and Protestant leaders can meet together in an atmosphere of great freedom.

All of us believe in the word of God and in

the importance of living it, even though, at times, our interpretation of it might differ. We seek to stress what we have in common, while remaining loyal to our respective Churches and their particular beliefs and traditions. The Holy Spirit seems to be blessing these good intentions. Thus, at the grass roots level, a common foundation is being established, and we are all discovering that much more unites us than divides us.

There is a mutual enrichment taking place as well. For instance, we Catholics have always believed in the word of God, but we must sincerely admit that our contact with Protestants has increased our esteem for it, and heightened our awareness of the word of God as a presence of Christ. And on their part, for instance, it seems to me that our Protestant friends now have fewer misgivings about our devotion to Mary. They love her as the perfect Christian and understand that although she is a human being, she is special.

With people of other religions, we also try to emphasize what unites us; and here, too, there is much. Take the Muslims, for instance, who believe in Mohammed and in the Koran, their holy book. They, too, when they get to know our Movement, often feel urged to "live" their religion more. So they look in the Koran for sentences as similar as possible to our "Words of Life" and try to put them into practice. They, too, believe in God as the All-Merciful, and hold to many truths which are similar to ours. Thus a common basis is being created.

Similar experiences resulted when we came in contact with the Rissho Kosei Kai, a vast Buddhist movement which has more than four million members. And the same is happening now with Jewish people, especially in North America. However, this is more understandable because we have the Old Testament in common with them. We have also found a bond with many animists in Africa because we have in common a faith in Someone who transcends us.

In addition, our Movement has activities aimed at helping people in the Third World, or at working for peace or other goals. Everyone can work together for these goals. This coming together to work for the good of people in need gradually destroys old prejudices and generates mutual esteem.

I understand that it is possible, at least to some degree, for Christians to achieve unity

and understanding with those of non-Christian faiths; but do you think it is ever possible to learn spiritual truths from non-Christians?

I think it is, because they are all human beings created in the image of God. And all of us, as human beings, have the vocation to be in communion with God, who has not forgotten anyone. Therefore, it is always possible to learn some truth from non-Christians, although this truth is already entirely present in Jesus Christ.

Do you have a personal experience, or do you know of one involving someone else, in which a Christian may have learned something from a non-Christian, some spiritual truth which he or she may not have known before?

Certainly. In our contacts with Muslims, for instance, we have learned from the solidarity we find among them. To them, the witness of an individual Christian doesn't mean anything. A collective witness is necessary. They remind us that Christianity is communion.

Cardinal Suenens has said in his *New Pentecost* that he wished he knew more about your contacts and relationship with Athenagoras, the late Patriarch of Constantinople. I know that Athenagoras called himself a Focolarino; but I wonder if you could tell me a little more about that relationship and what you learned from it.

Patriarch Athenagoras was the one who revealed to us the beauty of the Orthodox Church. From him we understood that the Eastern Church emphasizes life; that is, truth translated into life. And we also understood how important the Orthodox consider love.

But I had a deep rapport with the Patriarch also because of the fact that I knew Pope Paul VI very well, having known him since 1951 or 1952. Because it was possible for me to have a personal contact with the Pope, I unintentionally became a means for the Patriarch to communicate with the Pope in an unofficial way.

The Patriarch's great aspiration was to re-establish unity with the Catholic Church, after one thousand years of separation. I often conveyed his aspirations, thoughts, and sentiments to Pope Paul. This contributed to cementing the unity between these two Church leaders. Patriarch Athenagoras was ready to do anything in order to reach "one chalice." And Pope Paul developed a tremendous esteem for him; so much so, that when the Patriarch died, the Pope said: "A saint has died."

Athenagoras possessed a spiritual richness that he was able to share with us Catholics as well.

How long did you know the Patriarch?

About seven years.

There is a tremendous emphasis, obviously, in the Focolare Movement on community or *koinonia*, as the term is used in the New Testament. What do you think are the fundamental elements to foster this kind of community or *koinonia* spirit?

The most perfect community, the one upon which we must model our life, is the Most Blessed Trinity, the community of the three Divine

Persons. The communitarian spirit we need to have is the same spirit that unites the three Divine Persons in one; and this spirit is communicated to us through baptism, when the Holy Spirit pours supernatural love into our hearts. Love is this communitarian spirit. In order to have true community, we need *that* love. Jesus said to the Father, "That they may be one *as you and I are one.*" And this means in the same way, and therefore with the same love.

Do you have any special time or place when you meet regularly with a small group of intimate Christian friends where you can share concerns and problems?

I do this with the people with whom I live, with the Coordinating Council of the Movement, and with those I meet, whether in large or small gatherings.

How large might one of these smaller groups be?

Two persons are enough, because Jesus said that where two or three are gathered in his name, he is there among them.

How often do you do this? Every day? Once or twice a week?

This is a life. This is the way we live all the time.

Is there ever any difficulty, when you are sharing in depth in a small group, in being able to tell other persons the truth about themselves and yet do it in a spirit of love?

I can tell you a little about how we do it. One of the things we share with one another are our personal experiences. For instance, in the Movement there are many Word of Life groups, which are composed of people of diverse backgrounds who meet together in order to share the effects of the Word of Life in their daily lives. But I must add that in our Movement it took years to learn to distinguish what should be shared and what can be shared, from what may be said only in private—to one's confessor, for instance. Because we must be prudent; and people should neither be scandalized nor obliged to risk their reputations.

Furthermore, we have always made it a practice to share only out of love, so as to avoid pride. From the very beginning, we were helped by the words of Scripture: "A king's secret it is prudent to keep. But the works of God are to be made known with due honor" (Tobit. 12:11). Naturally this is to be done when it is God's will and in the way he wants.

You said you had drawn a line, that there were certain things you felt were better said in private, with one's confessor...

Yes, that is so.

I am wondering if there are some guidelines that you follow. The reason I ask is that there might be other people from a non-Catholic tradition who are interested in knowing what things you have found that are not best revealed in a group?

Those things which could hurt a person's good name, either our own or someone else's; because everyone has a right to his or her good name.

From the very beginning it has been customary in our community to practice a sort of mutual correction, coupled with another practice which can be called mutual emulation. I don't remember how this practice came about, but certainly it was a fruit of love. We call this mutual correction and emulation the "moment of truth." It takes place especially among those who are at the core of the Movement; therefore, among the Focolarini, the Volunteers and the Gen. This is what happens: a small number of people meet with a person who is responsible for the group. In the Focolare it will be the head of the Focolare, in the Volunteer nucleus, the head of the nucleus, in the Gen unit, the head of the unit. Then, at the right moment, all say what they see as negative in each of the others. It must be said out of love, but sincerely. (One always has to keep in mind which things it is prudent to share.) Sometimes we draw straws to choose the person who is to be loved in this way. Then each member who is present says something that he or she has seen in that person, which, according to him or to her, is not in conformity with the Christian ideal that we want to live. At the end, the person who is responsible for the group corrects what he or she thinks was not exact in what has been said.

When this part is over, the second part starts, with the sharing of another aspect of the truth: the good that we see in the others. A name is drawn, and each one says something good that he or she has observed in this person.

What is most striking at the end of the "moment of truth" is the tremendous joy that this practice evokes. Just as a cold shower is invigorating and stimulates the circulation of the blood, so also this revelation of the truth about ourselves (of which, often, we have been unaware) causes the "blood"—the mutual love—of our little community to circulate more. We feel an increased presence of the Holy Spirit and a tremendous, indescribable joy. One has to experience it in order to understand it.

Is the "moment of truth" done regularly?

In the Focolare, once a week. With the Coordinating Council here, once a month, because it meets once a month. (In the Coordinating Council are the leaders of the whole Movement.)

When you say here, "Focolare," are you talking about the core group, or are you talking about everyone connected with it?

The core group.

So this would not necessarily take place with the thousands of others?

At the present moment, it does not. It does take place among the Volunteers and the Gen.

Is this something that has existed from the beginning?

Yes.

So back when you were in that little house in Trent?

Yes.

As a woman, who is the leader of a large Christian group that has both men and women in it, do you feel any sort of tension or conflict with the Scriptural approach to the role of women?

From Scripture we see that Jesus chose men as teachers, priests, and guides, as in the case of Peter and the Apostles, and of Paul. But not only men followed Jesus. His mother, Mary, and other women disciples were very close to him. Mary was full of grace; and she was in the Cenacle on Pentecost.

Mary's first task was to give life to Jesus. She is *Theotokos*, "Mother of God," because she is mother of the Word made flesh. But this first task does not preclude her having had other tasks as well. She was close to the apostles after Jesus' death. Jesus had entrusted her to John as his mother, and had entrusted John to her as her son. Certainly, Mary, who lived life fully, did not remain silent. She spoke, and the fullness of the Holy Spirit in her heart overflowed on those around her. We have an example of this in her meeting with Elizabeth, when Mary proclaimed the "Magnificat." Her service to the Church was not the same as that of the Apostles, who were to preach, to spread the word of God, to baptize, to found the Church. Her task was more the task of a mother, loving and supporting the Apostles and the infant Church. She did for the Church a little of what she had done for the child Jesus.

We think of Mary as filled with charisms. And certainly she made these bear fruit for the Church while she was still alive; otherwise, why would she have had them? It is true that there is not much about her in Scripture, but I believe that this was preordained by Providence. For Mary was not meant to distract us, in even a minimal way, from giving our full attention to the figure of Jesus. Although she was his mother, at the same time she was simply a created human being.

If we look at her example, and think of her as a model—a model which no one can ever fully relive—we will be able to understand the other women who, throughout the Church's history, have received charisms from God for the good of the Church and of humanity. These charisms have revitalized the Mystical Body of Christ, bringing about a greater presence of the Holy Spirit in ways suited to the needs of the times. Thus these women are, in some way, mothers; just as men so endowed are fathers. And, in fact, these women have often given the Church new religious families.

All God's gifts are love, but they are also light. Frequently, therefore, these charisms also contain a doctrine; that is, a particular way of viewing the Gospel that is in accord with the interpretation given by the teaching Church. Thus, women who have received such a charism from God are teachers; and, at times, the Church even considers them Doctors of the Church— like St. Catherine of Siena and St. Teresa of Avila. Thus they teach; but their teaching is, above all, a ministry of love and service.

There is a passage in 1 Timothy where Paul says that women shouldn't teach. Are you making a distinction between what you

are doing or what these other women were doing and what he was talking about? And would the distinction be in terms of what they're teaching, or the style?

I think that in the Church the Holy Spirit uses men in one way and women in another. The Spirit takes men and makes them bishops and shepherds, with the task of interpreting the Church's patrimony of truth, and so on. Men are used by the Spirit as shepherds and teachers; but in the case of women, it is a different story. Theirs is a teaching that comes from love; but it is nonetheless a teaching, and often a doctrine.

Some say that there should be a difference between the way men relate to men and women relate to women, in a Christian community, and it is therefore best that you don't have a mixed group; that you segregate the sexes for the best kind of community interaction—*koinonia* interaction. Do you think that this is so?

Yes and no. I see that at times it is good to have men and women in separate groups in order to create an atmosphere in which people can speak more freely, more profoundly. The affinity that exists between men and men, and women and women, makes this communion, this sharing, easier. Furthermore, our experience tells us that this is especially useful in the case of young people. For in this case, the reciprocal sentiments that could otherwise arise—and that elsewhere could be very useful, for instance, in helping to form a good Christian family—might interfere with the group's efforts to reach a full spiritual communion.

All the same, it is very useful, at times, to have mixed meetings because of the mutual enrichment, both supernatural and natural, that is possible when both men and women are present.

Some might say that the expressions of Christian love are too feminine or soft to be fully compatible with really effective leadership. What do you think about that?

I don't think that anyone has ever spoken in as strong or compelling a way as Jesus does. When he speaks of love, he certainly doesn't mean mere human sentiment, even though he himself was very rich in human feelings and burst into tears at the death of Lazarus. He means, primarily, a capacity for self-sacrifice and for giving one's life for others. However, when Jesus speaks with authority, as when he rebukes the scribes and pharisees with the words, "Woe to you..." "Woe to you..." etc., he is never authoritarian because when he speaks the truth, he does it out of love for those he is speaking to.

If the disciples or followers of a leader know that he or she loves them, when they are dealt with forcefully they accept the admonition as a gift.

C.S. Lewis wrote a book called *Surprised by Joy*, in which he indicated that most of his life he had been looking for joy, then all of a sudden, it came to him from a different direction. A lot of other people are looking for peace and joy. From your words, it would seem that you experience quite a bit of both. How did you find them?

There are a peace and a joy which are not of this world. This is something one has to experience. We began to experience it at the beginning of the Movement when we decided to do God's will, to make our will one with his will. We tried to live like this moment by moment, instant by instant. This way of life brought us great joy and great peace, but a peace and joy that are not of this world—that the world does not experience. So, too, when we tried to put into practice Jesus' New Commandment as an expression of God's will, we experienced peace, joy, and light. These are fruits of the Spirit, and their presence is particularly noticeable when there is unity.

What could we suggest to those who want to experience this joy?

It is to be found in mutual love. We should teach everyone to love one another. When Jesus spoke about unity, he spoke of the fullness of joy. And it's really true!

How important is your prayer life? Could you tell me something about it?

It is very important. Extremely important! My prayer life follows our Rule of life, which expresses what we have always felt to be God's will for us. Prayer is very important. It is our audience with God, the Father, the Son, and the Holy Spirit, and with Jesus in the Eucharist, as well as with Mary, the angels, and the saints. There we take care of all our "business." And whatever is straightened out there will afterward straighten itself out in our lives in the world.

How do you pray? Do you pray a lot?

It is not our practice to multiply our prayers, but rather, as St. Francis de Sales advises, to work at perfecting them. When I pray, I try to pay attention to each word, aware that I am speaking to someone.

How much time do you spend in prayer each day?

All told, I pray about two hours a day. We have morning and evening prayer, meditation, Mass, a visit to Jesus in the Eucharist, and we pray the rosary, meditating on the mysteries in the lives of Jesus and Mary. We avail ourselves of the grace of the Sacrament of Reconciliation every two weeks. Once a month we have a day of spiritual retreat, and once a year we have four or five days of spiritual exercises.

Do you spend a lot of time in contemplation or meditation? What method do you use?

I spend about a half hour in meditation each day. I let my heart lead me. It is an intimate dialogue with God. But this is also true of my other prayers.

Has the Focolare Movement met any resistance within the Catholic Church? If so, how have you resolved this problem?

For a Catholic, what the pope thinks is of primary importance. At times, there are works within the Church which are understood almost solely by the pope, who has the grace to approve them. For instance, in the case of the Blessed

Sacrament Fathers, it was the pope who understood the value of what they were. As for us, all the popes have always been favorable to the Movement. They all blessed it abundantly: Pius XII, John XXIII, Paul VI, John Paul I, and John Paul II. There have been difficulties at times—if you wish to call them difficulties—but these stemmed from the fact that the Movement was something rather new in the Church. Some saw in it a Protestant touch; others, a Communist touch because of the sharing of possessions.

Was it because of the emphasis on Scripture that Catholics said there was a Protestant element in the Movement?

No. Usually it was because years ago people were not too used to seeing lay people with charisms, even though there have been such persons throughout the history of the Church.

As for the "Communist" touch, that was the sharing of goods?

Yes. But these are just two examples of the difficulties we encountered. In other instances, it was we who had the defects of neophytes; and in those cases, criticism was justified.

How were all these difficulties worked out?

After carefully studying us, the Church formally approved the Movement and blessed us.

APPENDIX

Highlights in the history of the Focolare Movement

1943-Chiara Lubich consecrates her life to God
1944-First women's Focolare: Trent, Italy
1948-First men's Focolare: Trent, Italy
  -Igino Giordani becomes first married Focolarino
1949-First Mariapolis (Focolare summer gathering): Italy
1956-The branch of the "Volunteers for God" begins
  -First Focolare outside Italy: Brussels, Belgium
1958-First Focolares outside Europe: Brazil and Argentina
1959-Last single Mariapolis in Italy: 12,000 participants
1960-Ecumenical center *Centro Uno* opens in Rome
1961-Inauguration of International School of Formation for Focolarini: Rome
  -First Focolares in North America: New York

1962-Pope John XXIII officially approves the Focolare Movement
1963-First Mariapolis in North America: New Jersey
1964-Inauguration of the International School on the Focolare Spirituality for Diocesan Priests: Rome
   -Chiara Lubich visits Focolares in North America
   -First permanent Mariapolis founded in Loppiano, Italy
1966-Permanent Mariapolis begins in Fontem, Cameroon
   -The Archbishop of Canterbury, Michael Ramsey, receives Chiara Lubich in audience and encourages the spreading of the Movement among Anglicans
   -First Focolares in Asia: Manila, Philippines
   -First Focolare in Australia
1967-First of many audiences of Chiara Lubich with Patriarch Athenagoras I in Istanbul
   -The Gen Movement (youth section of the Focolare Movement) begins
1968-Chiara Lubich visits the Focolares in New York and Chicago. She founds the school of formation for American Focolarini
   -Mariapolis Center (center for formation in the Focolare spirituality) is inaugurated in Chicago
   -Permanent Mariapolis begins in O'Higgins, Argentina

1969-Inauguration of the Center for Ecumenical Life at Ottmaring, Germany
 -Permanent Mariapolis begins near Sao Paulo, Brazil
1970-Inauguration of the International School on the Focolare Spirituality for Women Religious: Rome
1973-First Gen Fest: Loppiano, Italy. 3,000 participants
1974-Permanent Mariapolis begins in Tagaytay, Philippines
1977-Chiara Lubich is awarded the Templeton Prize for Progress in Religion
 -Inauguration of the International School on the Focolare Spirituality for Men Religious: Rome
 -Two Mariapolises take place in North America: Oregon and New York
1978-Three Mariapolises take place in North America: Washington state, New Mexico, and New York
1980-Fourth Gen Fest: Rome. 50,000 participants
1981-Family Fest: Rome. 25,000 participants
 -Chiara Lubich is honored with the Order of Saint Augustine of Canterbury by the Archbishop of Canterbury, Robert Runcie, for her work "within and for the Anglican communion"
 -Inauguration of Ecumenical Schools for the members of the Movement in Great Britain, Germany, and the United States

- Permanent Mariapolis begins in Montet, Switzerland
- Chiara Lubich speaks about her Christian experience before 10,000 Buddhists in Tokyo, Japan
- Four Mariapolises take place in North America: Washington state, New Mexico, Wisconsin, and New York
- The Focolare Movement in North America celebrates its twentieth anniversary at a commemorative Mass in St. Patrick's Cathedral, New York, with 2,000 attending. Cardinal Cooke is main celebrant

1982
- World congress of 7,000 priests and men religious associated with the Focolare Movement takes place in Paul VI Hall, Rome. Participants from sixty countries. Pope John Paul II addresses them and is main celebrant at Mass described as largest concelebration in history
- Chiara Lubich founds the Focolare School for Dialogue with the Great Religions of Asia: Manila, Philippines

1983
- Inauguration of the Asian branch of the School on the Focolare Spirituality for Diocesan Priests: Tagaytay, Philippines
- International conference of the New Humanity section of the Focolare Movement: Rome. Pope John Paul II addresses 20,000 participants

The following books provide further information on the Focolare Movement:

- *May they All Be One, Origins and Life of the Focolare Movement*, Chiara Lubich (New City Press, New York), 1983
- *That the World May Believe, Chiara Lubich and the Focolare Movement*, Hugh J. Moran (New City Press, New York), 1983
- *Chiara*, Edwin Robertson (Christian Journals [Ireland] Limited), 1978
- *Focolare after Thirty Years*, N. Grimaldi and S.C. Lorit (New City Press, New York), 1976

These books, as well as Chiara Lubich's other writings are available from New City Press, 206 Skillman Avenue, Brooklyn, N.Y. 11211